Change
Happens.

A COMPENDIUM OF WISDOM

Change Happens.

KATHRYN & ROSS PETRAS

WORKMAN PUBLISHING | NEW YORK

Copyright © 2018 by Kathryn & Ross Petras

Library of Congress Cataloging-in-Publication Data is available.

ISBN 978-1-5235-0203-5

Design by Galen Smith
Illustrations by Rebecca Bradley

Workman books are available at special discounts when purchased in bulk for premiums and sales promotions as well as for fund-raising or educational use. Special editions or book excerpts can also be created to specification. For details, contact the Special Sales Director at the address below, or send an email to specialmarkets@workman.com.

Workman Publishing Co., Inc.
225 Varick Street
New York, NY 10014-4381
workman.com

WORKMAN is a registered trademark of Workman Publishing Co., Inc.

Printed in China
First printing February 2018

10 9 8 7 6 5 4 3 2 1

Contents

Introduction .... PAGE IX

A
PAGE XIV
accepting • *adapting*

B
PAGE 8
beauty of change • *the big picture*

C
PAGE 14
challenges • *chaos* • *control* • *coping*
• *creating* • *curveballs*

D
PAGE 26
daring • *discovering yourself* • *don't look back*
• *dreaming*

E
PAGE 32
embracing change • *evolution*

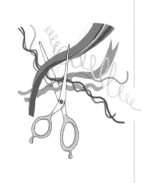

F PAGE 38
facing fears · faith · flexibility · fluidity

G PAGE 52
goals · going through the fire · growth

H PAGE 62
hard facts · hope

I PAGE 68
importance of change · incessantness of change

J PAGE 78
just do it

K PAGE 84
keeping your eyes open · keys to change

L PAGE 88
*letting go · life and change · the lighter side
of change · little things matter · loss*

M PAGE 98
making change happen · *making decisions to change*

N PAGE 104
natural rhythms · *necessity of change* · *new beginnings*

O PAGE 120
opportunity · *outlook*

P PAGE 128
paradoxes · *past* · *positive side of change* · *possibilities* · *preparation* · *present*

Q PAGE 142
quantum leaps

R PAGE 148
resisting change · *risk taking*

S PAGE 154
second chances · *seeking change* · *stagnation* · *surprises*

T   **PAGE 164**
     time · time for change · transience

U   **PAGE 172**
     unchanging center · unexpected

V   **PAGE 176**
     verities

W   **PAGE 186**
     welcoming change

X   **PAGE 194**
     xenophobia/xenophilia

Y   **PAGE 198**
     you

Z   **PAGE 204**
     zero hour

Introduction

Yes, change happens. We all know that. And we also know there's nothing we can do about it . . . or so we all too often think. But that's not necessarily the case.

Change is inevitable. Change has always happened and will always happen, and we can't stop it. And we have two options: We can try to resist it (and lose) or we can face it and grow with it. So there's really only one *good* option: to embrace change.

And that's what this book is designed to help you do.

We started collecting words of wisdom about change because the two of us have been through a series of major life changes—from the illness then death of our mother to moves (both of us in the same summer), from a cancer diagnosis to divorce and remarriage to unexpected business success, from moving to another country to the marriage of a child.

In fact, when we look back, we realize that the one constant in the past couple of years has been change. Some bad, some good, but all of it unavoidable. We had no choice but to go with the flow.

Of course, it wasn't always that easy. As poet Audre Lorde said, "Change means growth, and growth can be painful." But what helped us as avid curators of quotes was seeking out the insights and advice of other people who've faced change, embraced change, and grown because of it. These are people from across time and from around the world, people from all walks of life, ranging from Patti Smith to Rūmī, from Stephen Hawking to Maya Angelou. The insights and advice compiled here were companions for us on our journey from point A to point B, from the known to the unknown.

As with us, you'll find that sometimes the words will comfort you and remind you you're not alone. Other times, they'll galvanize you. Still other times they'll give you that peace at the center of all the flux around you. But they always will confirm one thing: You can do this. You can make that move, you can reach out into new areas. You can bear the unbearable changes, you can dive into new exciting possibilities. In short, you can change and you can change well. So really this book isn't just about change. It's about living your life to its best potential. For, as futurist Alvin Toffler said so succinctly: "Change is not merely necessary to life—it *is* life."

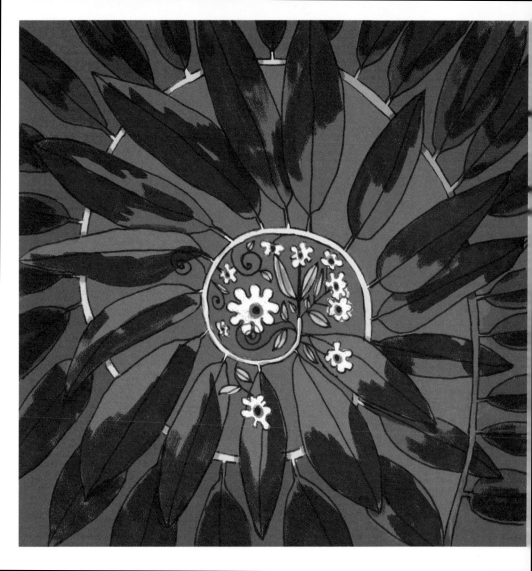

We're in a free fall into the future. We don't know where we're going. Things are changing so fast, and always when you're going through a long tunnel, anxiety comes along. And all you have to do to transform your hell into a paradise is to turn your fall into a voluntary act. It's a very interesting shift of perspective and that's all it is . . . joyful participation in the sorrows and everything changes.

–JOSEPH CAMPBELL
mythologist

A

accepting

adapting

I can change the story. I am the story. Begin.

–JEANETTE WINTERSON
writer

I don't know what has happened to the world, but you're up next in the batter's box.

–NEIL DEGRASSE TYSON
astrophysicist

I used to want to change the world. Now I'm open to letting it change me.

–PO BRONSON
journalist

Everything changes. As long as we live, we have to accept this truth without knowing. Without being aware of this truth, you cannot live in this world. Even though you try to escape from it, your effort is in vain.

–SHUNRYU SUZUKI
monk

adapting

You can't stop the waves, but you can learn to surf.

–OSEL TENDZIN
teacher

We should not try to alter circumstances but to adapt ourselves to them as they really are, just as sailors do. They don't try to change the winds or the sea but ensure that they are always ready to adapt themselves to conditions. In a flat calm they use the oars; with a following breeze they hoist full sail; in a head wind they shorten sail or heave to. Adapt yourself to circumstances in the same way.

–BION OF BORYSTHENES
philosopher

Adapt or perish, now as ever, is Nature's inexorable imperative.

–H. G. WELLS
writer

It is hard to adapt to chaos, but it can be done. I am living proof of that: It can be done.

—KURT VONNEGUT
writer

adapting

....

It is not the most intellectual of the species that survives; it is not the strongest that survives; but the species that survives is the one that is able to adapt to and to adjust best to the changing environment in which it finds itself.

–LEON C. MEGGINSON
professor

You learn more by adapting. When somebody has to adapt to you, you're not learning anything; they're learning it. But when you're doing the adapting, you find out more ways to do things.

–WES MONTGOMERY
jazz musician

Whosoever desires constant success must change his conduct with the times.

–NICCOLÒ MACHIAVELLI
historian/philosopher

Intelligence is the ability to adapt to change.

–STEPHEN HAWKING
physicist

adapting

....

When it is obvious that the goals cannot be reached, don't adjust the goals, adjust the action steps.

–CONFUCIUS
philosopher

adapting

The art of life is a constant readjustment to our surroundings.

–KAKUZO OKAKURA
writer

All living things contain a measure of madness that moves them in strange, sometimes inexplicable ways. This madness can be saving; it is part and parcel of the ability to adapt. Without it, no species would survive.

–YANN MARTEL
writer

B

beauty of change

the big picture

Change comes like a little wind that ruffles the curtains at dawn, and it comes like the stealthy perfume of wildflowers hidden in the grass.

—**JOHN STEINBECK**
writer

The reality is that we're all in the wilderness, and we have to survive on our own, and things constantly change and if we don't accept that, then we're just trying to fool ourselves. But the beauty of wilderness is that sometimes you can wake up in the morning and feel so sweet and whole.

—**SOPHIE B. HAWKINS**
musician

Even now, I still believe metamorphosis is the greatest beauty.

—**DAVID VANN**
writer

beauty of change

beauty
of change

. . . .

We are not trapped or locked up in these bones. No, no. We are free to change. And love changes us. And if we can love one another, we can break open the sky.

–WALTER MOSLEY
writer

After a great blow, or crisis, after the first shock and then after the nerves have stopped screaming and twitching, you settle down to the new condition of things and feel that all possibility of change has been used up. You adjust yourself, and are sure that the new equilibrium is for eternity. . . . But if anything is certain it is that no story is ever over, for the story which we think is over is only a chapter in a story which will not be over, and it isn't the game that is over, it is just an inning, and that game has a lot more than nine innings. When the game stops it will be called on account of darkness. But it is a long day.

–ROBERT PENN WARREN
writer

. . . .

It is almost banal to say so yet it needs to be stressed continually: all is creation, all is change, all is flux, all is metamorphosis.

–HENRY MILLER
writer

Change begets change. Nothing propagates so fast.

–CHARLES DICKENS
writer

Everything takes time. Bees have to move very fast to stay still.

–DAVID FOSTER WALLACE
writer

The universe is change; our life is what our thoughts make it.

–MARCUS AURELIUS
philosopher/emperor

All things change, and we change with them.

–MATTHIAS BORBONIUS
alchemist

Nothing endures but change.

–HERACLITUS
philosopher

The only thing that one really knows about human nature is that it changes. Change is the one quality we can predicate of it.

–OSCAR WILDE
writer

All things change, nothing perishes.

–OVID (PUBLIUS OVIDIUS NASO)
poet

C

challenges

chaos

control

coping

creating

curveballs

The dogmas of the quiet past are inadequate to the stormy present. The occasion is piled high with difficulty, and we must rise with the occasion. As our case is new, so we must think anew and act anew.

–**ABRAHAM LINCOLN**
president

Imagination is the voice of daring.

–**HENRY MILLER**
writer

Stepping onto a brand-new path is difficult, but not more difficult than remaining in a situation.

–**MAYA ANGELOU**
writer

When we are no longer able to change a situation . . . we are challenged to change ourselves.

–**VIKTOR FRANKL**
neurologist/psychiatrist

challenges
....

challenges

When we least expect it, life sets us a challenge to test our courage and willingness to change; at such a moment, there is no point in pretending that nothing has happened or in saying that we are not yet ready. The challenge will not wait. Life does not look back. A week is more than enough time for us to decide whether or not to accept our destiny.

–PAULO COELHO
writer

If you dare nothing, then when the day is over, nothing is all you will have gained.

–NEIL GAIMAN
writer

chaos

....

Life is nothing without a little chaos to make it interesting.

–AMELIA ATWATER-RHODES
writer

I tell you: one must still have chaos in one, to give birth to a dancing star. I tell you: you have still chaos in you.

–FRIEDRICH NIETZSCHE
philosopher

Chaos is a friend of mine. It's like I accept him; does he accept me?

–BOB DYLAN
musician

Our real discoveries come from chaos, from going to the place that looks wrong and stupid and foolish.

–CHUCK PALAHNIUK
writer

I finally figured out that not every crisis can be managed. . . . As much as we want to keep ourselves safe, we can't protect ourselves from everything. If we want to embrace life, we also have to embrace chaos.

–SUSAN ELIZABETH PHILLIPS
writer

Chaos contains information that can lead to knowledge—even wisdom.

–TONI MORRISON
writer

control

The control we believe we have is purely illusory . . . every moment we teeter on chaos and oblivion.

–**CLIVE BARKER**
writer

You are not controlling the storm, and you are not lost in it. You are the storm.

–**SAM HARRIS**
philosopher

coping

The business changes. The technology changes. The team changes. The team members change. The problem isn't change, per se, because change is going to happen; the problem, rather, is the inability to cope with change when it comes.

–**KENT BECK**
software engineer

Life is easier than you'd think; all that is necessary is to accept the impossible, do without the indispensable, and bear the intolerable.

–KATHLEEN THOMPSON NORRIS
writer

If you can't laugh when things go bad—laugh and put on a little carnival—then you're either dead or wishing you were.

–STEPHEN KING
writer

creating

The world is more malleable than you think and it's
waiting for you to hammer it into shape.

–BONO
singer

If things are not failing, you are not innovating
enough.

–ELON MUSK
inventor/entrepreneur

Write it. Shoot it. Publish it. Crochet it, sauté it,
whatever. MAKE.

–JOSS WHEDON
film director/screenwriter

Invention, it must be humbly admitted, does not
consist in creating out of void, but out of chaos.

–MARY SHELLEY
writer

It wasn't about standing still and becoming safe. If anybody wants to keep creating they have to be about change.

–MILES DAVIS
jazz musician

Sometimes, you have to manufacture your own history. Give fate a push, so to speak.

–SARAH DESSEN
writer

A vase is begun; why, as the wheel goes round, does it turn out a pitcher?

–HORACE
poet

I feel confident imposing change on myself. It's a lot more fun progressing than looking back. That's why I need to throw curveballs.

–DAVID BOWIE
musician

It reminded me that pain was necessary. Pain was life's curveball. Without it, we would never appreciate what it felt like to be loved.

–S. L. JENNINGS
writer

D

daring

discovering yourself

don't look back

dreaming

What is the worst that could happen? It gets turned down by every publisher in Britain, big deal.

–J. K. ROWLING
writer

A ship in harbor is safe, but that is not what ships are made for.

–JOHN AUGUSTUS SHEDD
writer/professor

What would you do if you weren't afraid?

–SPENCER JOHNSON
writer

discovering yourself

Have I given myself permission to completely change the way my life would've gone? Have I given myself permission to not be who I thought I might have turned into? Or have I, in fact, actually just turned into the person I always should've been?

–DAVID BOWIE
musician

What you are thinking about, you are becoming.

–MUHAMMAD ALI
boxer

We go through life. We shed our skins. We become ourselves.

–PATTI SMITH
musician/writer

You will go down many paths that go nowhere. . . .
You will try things on and realize they don't fit. And
that's how it should be.

–ANDERSON COOPER
news anchor

don't look back

In times of rapid change, experience could be your worst enemy.

–J. PAUL GETTY
business executive

You can never plan the future by the past.

–EDMUND BURKE
statesman

dreaming

We dream to give ourselves hope. To stop dreaming— well, that's like saying you can never change your fate.

–AMY TAN
writer

Thankfully, dreams can change. If we'd all stuck with our first dream, the world would be overrun with cowboys and princesses.

–STEPHEN COLBERT
comedian/talk show host

Throw your dream into space like a kite, and you do not know what it will bring back, a new life, a new friend, a new love, a new country.

–ANAÏS NIN
writer

Dreams ahead/proceed with determination

–LINH DINH
columnist (who saw this sign on a bike advertising Big Mouth Ben's Atlanta convenience store)

E

embracing
change

evolution

The only way to make sense out of change is to plunge into it, move with it, and join the dance.

–ALAN WATTS
philosopher

If I can't stay where I am, and I can't, then I will put all that I can into the going.

–JEANETTE WINTERSON
writer

Try new recipes, learn from your mistakes, be fearless, and above all have fun!

–JULIA CHILD
chef

embracing change

The biggest risk is not taking any risk. In a world that's changing really quickly, the only strategy that is guaranteed to fail is not taking risks.

–MARK ZUCKERBERG
entrepreneur

Every morning I jump out of bed and step on a landmine. The landmine is me. After the explosion, I spend the rest of the day putting the pieces together.

–RAY BRADBURY
writer

Some people don't like change, but you need to embrace change if the alternative is disaster.

–ELON MUSK
inventor/entrepreneur

The joy of life comes from our encounters with new experiences, and hence there is no greater joy than to have an endlessly changing horizon, for each day to have a new and different sun.

–JON KRAKAUER
writer/mountaineer

Tomorrow to fresh woods, and pastures new.

–JOHN MILTON
poet

....

embracing change

evolution

....

We delight in the beauty of the butterfly, but rarely admit the changes it has gone through to achieve that beauty.

–MAYA ANGELOU
writer

All things must change
To something new, to something strange.

–HENRY WADSWORTH LONGFELLOW
poet

It is not the conscious changes made in their lives by men and women—a new job, a new town, a divorce—which really shape them, like the chapter headings in a biography, but a long slow mutation of emotion, hidden, all-penetrative.

–NADINE GORDIMER
writer

To exist is to change, to change is to mature, to mature is to go on creating oneself endlessly.

–HENRI BERGSON
philosopher

Everyone needs a chance to evolve.

–JAY-Z
musician/businessman

F

facing fears

faith

flexibility

fluidity

The changes we dread most may contain our salvation.

–BARBARA KINGSOLVER
writer

I have accepted fear as part of life—specifically the fear of change. . . . I have gone ahead despite the pounding in the heart that says: turn back.

–ERICA JONG
writer

Taking a new step, uttering a new word, is what they fear most.

–FYODOR DOSTOYEVSKY
writer

facing fears

facing fears

People search for certainty. But there *is* no certainty. People are terrified—how can you live *and not know*? It is not odd at all. You only think you know, as a matter of fact. And most of your actions are based on incomplete knowledge and you really don't know what it is all about, or what the purpose of the world is, or know a great deal of other things. It is possible to live and not know.

—**RICHARD FEYNMAN**
physicist

Fear tastes like a rusty knife and do not let her into your house.

—**JOHN CHEEVER**
writer

The very cave you are afraid to enter turns out to be the source of what you are looking for. The damned thing in the cave that was so dreaded has become the center.

—**JOSEPH CAMPBELL**
mythologist

I'm not afraid of storms, for I'm learning how to sail my ship.

–**LOUISA MAY ALCOTT**
writer

facing fears

She had just realized there were two things that prevent us from achieving our dreams: believing them to be impossible or seeing those dreams made possible by some sudden turn of the wheel of fortune, when you least expected it. For at that moment, all our fears suddenly surface: the fear of setting off along a road heading who knows where, the fear of a life full of new challenges, the fear of losing forever everything that is familiar.

–PAULO COELHO
writer

There are no grounds for fear of the unknown: for often the things we most dreaded, before we experienced them, turn out to be better than those we desired.

–RENÉ DESCARTES
philosopher

[There is] a "negative path" to happiness that entails taking a radically different stance towards those things most of us spend our lives trying hard to avoid. This involves learning to enjoy uncertainty, embracing insecurity and becoming familiar with failure. In order to be truly happy, it turns out, we might actually need to be willing to experience more negative emotions— or, at the very least, to stop running quite so hard from them.

–OLIVER BURKEMAN
journalist

Do the scary thing first, and get scared later.

–LEMONY SNICKET
writer

You will never succeed unless you
let go of your fears and fly.

–RICHARD BRANSON
entrepreneur

Happiness means taking risks. And if you're not a little scared, you're not doing it right.

–SARAH ADDISON ALLEN
writer

The fishermen know that the sea is dangerous and the storm fearsome, but could never see that the dangers were a reason to continue strolling on the beach. They leave that wisdom to those to whom it appeals. When the storm comes—when night falls—what's worse: the danger or the fear of danger? Give me reality, the danger itself.

–VINCENT VAN GOGH
artist

facing fears

trust your heart
if the seas catch fire

–E. E. CUMMINGS
poet

faith

faith

. . . .

Faith is taking the first step even when you don't see the whole staircase.

–MARTIN LUTHER KING JR. (PARAPHRASED)
minister/activist

Change, indeed, is painful; yet ever needful; and if Memory have its force and worth, so also has Hope.

–THOMAS CARLYLE
philosopher

You need a leap of faith to leave your old life behind. True metamorphosis doesn't come with flowcharts.

–DAVID MITCHELL
writer

. . . .

When events change, I change my mind. What do you do?

–PAUL SAMUELSON
economist

I make up the rules of a game and I play it. If I seem to be losing, I change the rules.

–MICHAEL SNOW
artist

flexibility

flexibility

Life requires of man spiritual elasticity, so that he may temper his efforts to the chances that are offered.

–VIKTOR FRANKL
neurologist/psychiatrist

Real life is about reacting quickly to the opportunity at hand, not the opportunity you envisioned. Not thinking and scheming for the future, but letting it happen.

–CONAN O'BRIEN
humorist/talk show host

fluidity

When the music changes, so does the dance.

–AFRICAN PROVERB

Don't get set into one form, adapt it and build your own, and let it grow, be like water. Empty your mind, be formless, shapeless—like water. Now you put water in a cup, it becomes the cup; you put water into a bottle it becomes the bottle; you put it in a teapot it becomes the teapot. Now water can flow or it can crash. Be water, my friend.

–BRUCE LEE
martial artist

The world is like a Mask dancing. If you want to see it well, you do not stand in one place.

–CHINUA ACHEBE
writer

fluidity

Stay fluid and roll with those changes. Life is just a big extended improvisation.

–JANE LYNCH
actress

There are two kinds of people. . . . One kind, you can just tell by looking at them at what point they congealed into their final selves. It might be a very nice self, but you know you can expect no more surprises from it. Whereas, the other kind keep moving, changing. . . . They are *fluid*. They keep moving forward and making new trysts with life, and the motion of it keeps them young. In my opinion, they are the only people who are still alive. You must be constantly on your guard against congealing.

–GAIL GODWIN
writer

G

goals

*going through
the fire*

growth

Without effort and change, human life cannot remain good. It is not a finished Utopia that we ought to desire, but a world where imagination and hope are alive and active.

–BERTRAND RUSSELL
philosopher

The secret of change is to focus all your energy, not on fighting the old, but on building the new.

–DAN MILLMAN
gymnast

One is always nearer by not keeping still.

–THOM GUNN
poet

going through the fire

Crisis is unavoidable. Every human life seems to be drawn eventually, as if by some unspoken parallel, some tidal flow or underground magnetic field, toward the raw, dynamic essentials of its existence, as if everything up to that point had been a preparation for a meeting, for a confrontation in an elemental form with our essential flaw, and with what an individual could until then, only receive stepped down, interpreted or diluted.

This experience . . . where the touchable rawness of life becomes part of the fabric of the everyday, and a robust luminous vulnerability, becomes shot through with the necessary, imminent and inevitable prospect of loss, has been described for centuries as the dark night of the soul: *La noche oscura del alma.* But perhaps, this dark night could be more accurately described as the meeting of two immense storm fronts, the squally vulnerable edge between what overwhelms human beings from the inside and what overpowers them from the outside.

–DAVID WHYTE
poet/philosopher

*going
through
the fire*

*going
through
the fire*

Only after disaster can we be resurrected. "It's only after you've lost everything," Tyler says, "that you're free to do anything" . . . Nothing is static. Everything is falling apart.

—CHUCK PALAHNIUK
writer

There is in the worst of fortune the best of chances for a happy change.

–EURIPIDES
playwright

I have noticed that doing the sensible thing is only a good idea when the decision is quite small. For the life-changing things you must risk it.

And here is the shock—when you risk it, when you do the right thing, when you arrive at the borders of common sense and cross into unknown territory, leaving behind you all the familiar smells and lights, then you do not experience great joy and huge energy.

You are unhappy. Things get worse.

It is a time of mourning. Loss. Fear. We bullet ourselves through with questions. And then we feel shot and wounded.

And then all the cowards come out and say, "See, I told you so."

In fact, they told you nothing.

–JEANETTE WINTERSON
writer

*going
through
the fire*

going through the fire

Change always involves a dark night when everything falls apart. Yet if this period of dissolution is used to create new meaning, then chaos ends and new order emerges.

–MARGARET WHEATLEY
writer/management consultant

Desperation is the raw material of drastic change. Only those who can leave behind everything they have ever believed in can hope to escape.

–WILLIAM BURROUGHS
writer

It's not that I believe everything happens for a reason. . . . It's just that . . . I just think that some things are meant to be broken. Imperfect. Chaotic. It's the universe's way of providing contrast, you know? There have to be a few holes in the road. It's how life *is*.

–SARAH DESSEN
writer

growth

Change means growth, and growth can be painful.

–AUDRE LORDE
writer/activist

If we don't change, we don't grow. If we don't grow, we are not really living.

–GAIL SHEEHY
writer

In chaos, there is fertility.

–ANAÏS NIN
writer

When you stop growing you start dying.

—WILLIAM BURROUGHS
writer

H

hard facts

hope

We are taught you must blame your father, your sisters, your brothers, the school, the teachers—you can blame anyone, but never blame yourself. It's never your fault. But it's ALWAYS your fault, because if you wanted to change, you're the one who has got to change.

–KATHARINE HEPBURN
actress/writer

We want things we cannot have. We seek to reclaim a certain moment, sound, sensation. I want to hear my mother's voice. I want to see my children as children. Hands small, feet swift. Everything changes. Boy grown, father dead, daughter taller than me, weeping from a bad dream. Please stay forever, I say to the things I know. Don't go. Don't grow.

–PATTI SMITH
musician/writer

Sometimes if something is missing it has to be replaced by something else. It can't be helped.

–ROLANDO HINOJOSA-SMITH
writer

Change is not made without inconvenience, even from worse to better.

–RICHARD HOOKER
theologian

Those who expect moments of change to be comfortable and free of conflict have not learned their history.

–JOAN WALLACH SCOTT
historian

This is an important lesson to remember when you're having a bad day, a bad month, or a sh***y year. Things will change: you won't feel this way forever. And anyway, sometimes the hardest lessons to learn are the ones your soul needs most. I believe you can't feel real joy unless you've felt heartache. You can't have a sense of victory unless you know what it means to fail. You can't know what it's like to feel holy until you know what it's like to feel really f****** evil. And you can't be birthed again until you've died.

–KELLY CUTRONE
publicist/writer

hope

What I like most about change is that it's a synonym for "hope." If you are taking a risk, what you are really saying is "I believe in tomorrow and I will be part of it."

–LINDA ELLERBEE
journalist

Hope is an embrace of the unknown and the unknowable, an alternative to the certainty of both optimists and pessimists. Optimists think it will all be fine without our involvement; pessimists take the opposite position; both excuse themselves from acting.

–REBECCA SOLNIT
writer

I

*importance
of change*

*incessantness of
change*

It is in changing that things find purpose.

–HERACLITUS
philosopher

We must always change, renew, rejuvenate ourselves;
otherwise we harden.

**–JOHANN WOLFGANG VON
GOETHE**
writer

You say: the real, the world as it is. But it is not, it
becomes! It moves, it changes! It doesn't wait for us
to change. . . . It is more mobile than you can imagine.
You are getting closer to this reality when you say
as it "presents itself"; that means that it is not there,
existing as an object.

The world, the real is not an object. It is a process.

–JOHN CAGE
composer

*importance
of change*

I cannot say whether things will get better if we change; what I can say is they must change if they are to get better.

**–ATTRIBUTED TO
GEORG C. LICHTENBERG**
scientist/satirist

The foolish and the dead alone never change their opinion.

–JAMES RUSSELL LOWELL
poet/critic

Maybe curiosity killed the cat, but the lack of curiosity will kill us.

–PATTI SMITH
musician/writer

Everything is in a process of change. Nothing endures; we do not seek permanence.

–MASATOSHI NAITO
photographer

Change is constant.

–BENJAMIN DISRAELI
politician/writer

Evolution did not end with us growing thumbs. You do know that, right?

–BILL HICKS
comedian

I'm trying to play the truth of what I am. The reason it's difficult is because I'm changing all the time.

–CHARLES MINGUS
jazz musician

incessantness of change

incessantness of change

Change is the constant and we are constantly in change.

–CHRISTINA BALDWIN
writer

Human beings are works in progress that mistakenly think they're finished.

–DAN GILBERT
Harvard psychologist

Change alone is eternal, perpetual, immortal.

–ATTRIBUTED TO ARTHUR SCHOPENHAUER
philosopher

Time is a dressmaker specializing in alterations.

–FAITH BALDWIN
writer

Everything remains unsettled forever, depend on it.

–HENRY MILLER
writer

You could not step twice into the same river.

–HERACLITUS
philosopher

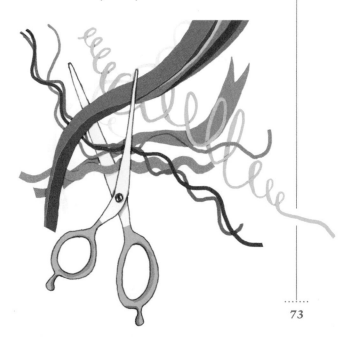

incessantness of change

We think of life as a solid and are haunted when time tells us it is a fluid. Old Heraclitus couldn't have stepped in the same river once, let alone twice.

–JIM HARRISON
writer

People were rivers, always ready to move from one state of being into another. It was not fair, she felt, to treat people as if they were finished beings. Everyone was always becoming and unbecoming.

–KATHLEEN WINTER
writer

Really there is no normal. There's only change, and resistance to it, and then more change.

–MERYL STREEP
actress

As wave is driven by wave
And each, pursued, pursues the wave ahead,
So time flies on and follows, flies and follows,
Always, for ever and new. What was before
Is left behind; what never was is now;
And every passing moment is renewed.

–OVID (PUBLIUS OVIDIUS NASO)
poet

Woe unto you the day it is said that you are finished!
To finish a work? To finish a picture? What nonsense!
To finish it means to be through with it, to kill it,
to rid it of its soul, to give it its final blow: the most
unfortunate one for the painter as well as for the
picture.

–PABLO PICASSO
artist

*incessantness
of change*

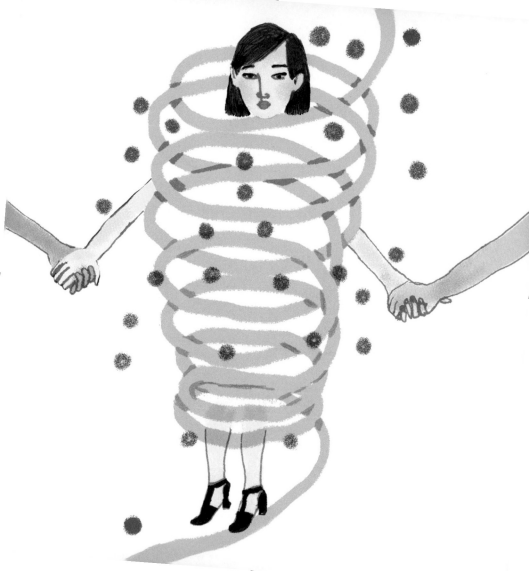

The life of man is a self-evolving circle, which, from a ring imperceptibly small, rushes on all sides outwards to new and larger circles, and that without end.

–RALPH WALDO EMERSON
essayist

Life's picture is constantly undergoing change.
The spirit beholds a new world every moment.

–JALĀL AD-DĪN AR-RŪMĪ
poet/mystic

Without change, something sleeps inside of us and seldom awakens.

–DAVID LYNCH
screenwriter/director

incessantness of change

J

just do it

I take pleasure in my transformations. I look quiet and consistent, but few know how many women there are in me.

–ANAÏS NIN
writer

It isn't true that you only live once. You only die once. You live lots of times if you know how.

–BOBBY DARIN
singer/songwriter

All your life you're yellow. Then one day you brush up against something blue, the barest touch, and voila, the rest of your life you're green.

–TESS CALLAHAN
writer

My life didn't please me, so I created my life.

–COCO CHANEL
fashion designer

just do it

The very fact of growing older means taking up a new business; all our circumstances change, and we must either stop doing anything at all or else willing and consciously take on the new role we have to play on life's stage.

–JOHANN WOLFGANG VON GOETHE
writer

Whenever they rebuild an old building, they must first of all destroy the old one.

–JALĀL AD-DĪN AR-RŪMĪ
poet/mystic

When I find myself at that point, in the position of someone who would change something—at that point I don't change it, I change myself. It's for that reason that I have said that instead of self-expression, I'm involved in self-alteration.

–JOHN CAGE
composer

I have forced myself to contradict myself in order to avoid conforming to my own taste.

–MARCEL DUCHAMP
artist

You can't go back and make a new start, but you can start right now and make a brand-new ending.

–JAMES R. SHERMAN
writer

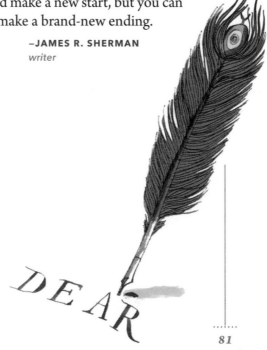

DE AR

just do it

....

Change is never perfect. Change means reinvention, and until something is reinvented, we have no idea what the spec is.

–SETH GODIN
writer/entrepreneur

....

Be like the fox
who makes more tracks than
        necessary,
some in the wrong direction.

–WENDELL BERRY
writer/environmental activist

....

K

keeping your eyes open

keys to change

If something is going to happen to me, I want to be there.

–ALBERT CAMUS
writer

Observe always that everything is the result of a change, and get used to thinking that there is nothing Nature loves so well as to change existing forms and to make new ones like them.

–MARCUS AURELIUS
philosopher/emperor

. . . .

All is connected . . . no one thing can change by itself.

–PAUL HAWKEN
environmentalist

*keeping
your eyes
open*

. . . .

*keys to
change*

. . . .

keys to change

....

If you don't like how things are, change it!
You're not a tree.

–JIM ROHN
entrepreneur

In a chronically leaking boat, energy devoted to
changing vessels is likely to be more productive than
energy devoted to patching leaks.

–WARREN BUFFETT
investor

Everything changes; everything is connected;
pay attention.

–JANE HIRSHFIELD
poet

No one is alone, and each change here brings about another change there. No one is alone and nothing is solid: change is comprised of fixities that are momentary accords.

–OCTAVIO PAZ
writer

Our meaning of happiness is constantly shaped and reshaped by small choices we make every day.

–JENNIFER AAKER
social psychologist

L

letting go

life and change

the lighter side
of change

little things
matter

loss

I don't know why we long so for permanence, why the fleeting nature of things so disturbs. With futility, we cling to the old wallet long after it has fallen apart. We visit and revisit the old neighborhood where we grew up, searching for the remembered grove of trees and the little fence. We clutch our old photographs. In our churches and synagogues and mosques, we pray to the everlasting and eternal. Yet, in every nook and cranny, nature screams at the top of her lungs that nothing lasts, that it is all passing away. All that we see around us, including our own bodies, is shifting and evaporating and one day will be gone.

–ALAN LIGHTMAN
physicist

Change is the only constant. Hanging on is the only sin.

–DENISE MCCLUGGAGE
auto racing driver/journalist

letting go

It's hard to embrace the future if you are continually holding on to who you used to be.

—JODIE FOSTER
film director/actress

Abandon yesterday.

—PETER DRUCKER
management consultant

life and change

I like to be the right thing in the wrong space and the wrong thing in the right space. . . . Being the right thing in the wrong space and the wrong thing in the right space is worth it, because something funny always happens.

—ANDY WARHOL
artist

The one constant in our life is change.

—DAN GILBERT
Harvard psychologist

Life changes in the instant. The ordinary instant.

–JOAN DIDION
writer

Change is not merely necessary to life—it *is* life.

–ALVIN TOFFLER
futurist

. . . .

Everything in life that we really accept undergoes a change.

–KATHERINE MANSFIELD
writer

. . . .

Just when I discovered the meaning of life, they changed it.

–GEORGE CARLIN
comedian

If you're in a bad situation, don't worry, it'll change. If you're in a good situation, don't worry, it'll change.

–JOHN A. SIMONE SR.
writer

Love can change a person the way a parent can change a baby— awkwardly, and often with a great deal of mess.

–LEMONY SNICKET
writer

Change is inevitable—except from a vending machine.

–ROBERT C. GALLAGHER
*businessman/former director of the
Green Bay Packers*

the lighter side of change

I'm not absolutely certain of my facts, but I rather fancy it's Shakespeare . . . who says that it's always just when a chappie is feeling particularly . . . braced with things in general that Fate sneaks up behind him with a bit of lead piping.

–P. G. WODEHOUSE
writer

I haven't the slightest idea how to change people, but still I keep a long list of prospective candidates just in case I should ever figure it out.

–DAVID SEDARIS
humorist

And that is how change happens. One gesture.
One person. One moment at a time.

–LIBBA BRAY
writer

Even very little things can change your destiny and
throw you to a different path, to a different fate; you
must never forget that even very little things have
great powers!

–MEHMET MURAT ILDAN
writer

Time and reflection change the sight little by little,
till we come to understand.

–PAUL CÉZANNE
artist

*little things
matter*

little things matter

Know what's weird? Day by day nothing seems to change, but pretty soon, everything is different.

–BILL WATTERSON
cartoonist

I am a believer in change *peu à peu* ("little by little") since drastic changes, including lots of changes made all at once, are often the sort of modifications that don't stick.

–MIREILLE GUILIANO
writer

loss

Unless you are prepared to give up something valuable, you will never be able to truly change at all, because you'll be forever in the control of things that you can't give up.

–ANDY LAW
writer

All changes, even the most longed for, have their melancholy; for what we leave behind us is a part of ourselves; we must die to one life before we can enter into another!

–ANATOLE FRANCE
writer

M
making change happen

making decisions to change

They always say that time changes things, but you actually have to change them yourself.

—**ANDY WARHOL**
artist

Not everything that is faced can be changed; but nothing can be changed until it is faced.

—**JAMES BALDWIN**
writer

In times such as ours, however, when there is too much order, too much management, too much programming and control, it becomes the duty of superior men and women to fling their favorite monkey wrenches into the machinery. To relieve the repression of the human spirit, they must sow doubt and disruption.

—**TOM ROBBINS**
writer

making change happen

making decisions to change

Most of us overestimate the value of what we currently have, and have to give up, and underestimate the value of what we may gain.

–JAMES BELASCO AND RALPH STAYER
business executives

Everything tells me that I am about to make a wrong decision, but making mistakes is just part of life. What does the world want of me? Does it want me to take no risks, to go back to where I came from because I didn't have the courage to say "yes" to life?

–PAULO COELHO
writer

Indecision is also a species of fear that, holding the soul, as it were, in suspense between several actions it might carry out, causes it to perform none of them, and thus gives it the time to make a proper choice before opting for one of them. In which respect, it is genuinely of some use. But when it lasts longer than it should, and causes us to squander on deliberation the time we need in order to act, it is very bad.

–RENÉ DESCARTES
philosopher

making
decisions
to change

Don't turn away from possible futures before you're certain you don't have anything to learn from them.

–RICHARD BACH
writer

Today is only one day in all the days that will ever be. But what will happen in all the other days that ever come can depend on what you do today.

–ERNEST HEMINGWAY
writer

N

natural rhythms

necessity of change

new beginnings

If you want to be a butterfly, you have to spend some time as a worm.

–BILL MAHER
humorist

All is change; all yields its place and goes.

–EURIPIDES
playwright

The world was changing, and it wouldn't change back.

–JACK CADY
writer

natural rhythms

Nothing ceases to exist—there is no example of this in nature. . . . There is an entire mass of things that cannot rationally be explained. There are newborn thoughts that have not yet found form. How foolish to deny the existence of the soul. After all, that a life has begun, that cannot be denied. It is necessary to believe in immortality, insofar as it can be demonstrated that the atoms of life or the spirit of life must continue to exist after the body's death. But of what does it exist, this characteristic of holding a body together, causing matter to change and develop, this spirit of life? I felt it as a sensual delight that I should become one with— become this earth which is forever radiated by the sun in a constant ferment and which lives—lives—and which will grow plants from my decaying body—trees and flowers—and the sun will warm them and I will exist in them—and nothing will perish—and that is eternity.

—EDVARD MUNCH
artist

The empty blue sky of space says, "All this comes back to me, then goes again, and comes back again, then goes again, and I don't care, it still belongs to me."

–JACK KEROUAC
writer

No one knows what your life or life itself should be because it is in the process of being created. Life moves according to a growing consciousness of life and is completely unpredictable.

–AGNES MARTIN
artist

··

When the moon is full, it begins to wane.

–JAPANESE PROVERB

··

natural rhythms

....

There are as many worlds as there are kinds of days, and as an opal changes its colors and its fire to match the nature of a day, so do I.

–JOHN STEINBECK
writer

Motion or change, and identity or rest, are the first and second secrets of nature: Motion and Rest. The whole code of her laws may be written on the thumbnail, or the signet of a ring.

–RALPH WALDO EMERSON
essayist

No one wants to die. Even people who want to go to heaven don't want to die to get there. And yet death is the destination we all share. No one has ever escaped it. And that is as it should be, because Death is very likely the single best invention of Life. It is Life's change agent. It clears out the old to make way for the new.

–STEVE JOBS
entrepreneur

necessity of change

. . . .

It may be hard for an egg to turn into a bird: it would be a jolly sight harder for it to learn to fly while remaining an egg. We are like eggs at present. And you cannot go on indefinitely being just an ordinary, decent egg. We must be hatched or go bad.

–C. S. LEWIS
writer

He that will not apply new remedies must expect new evils; for time is the greatest innovator.

–FRANCIS BACON
philosopher

Even as you search, you, yourself, are being changed, and you will understand that you must continue to change or die.

–ELDRIDGE CLEAVER
activist

The snake which cannot cast its skin perishes. As well the minds which are prevented from changing their opinions; they cease to be mind.

–FRIEDRICH NIETZSCHE
philosopher

Being stale is death.

–JERRY GARCIA
musician

You might be tempted to avoid the messiness of daily living for the tranquility of stillness and peacefulness. This of course would be an attachment to stillness, and like any strong attachment, it leads to delusion. It arrests development and short-circuits the cultivation of wisdom.

–JON KABAT-ZINN
writer

necessity of change

necessity of change

....

If you don't like change, you're going to like irrelevance even less.

–U.S. ARMY GENERAL ERIC SHINSEKI

That's your responsibility as a person, as a human being—to constantly be updating your positions on as many things as possible. And if you don't contradict yourself on a regular basis, then you're not thinking.

–MALCOLM GLADWELL
journalist

My view is that if your philosophy is not unsettled daily then you are blind to all the universe has to offer.

–NEIL DEGRASSE TYSON
astrophysicist

We can't become what we need to be by remaining what we are.

–MAX DE PREE
leadership expert

necessity of change

. . . .

But what if your fire is not burning well or, worse, has gone out? Without inner fire, you have no light, no heat, no desire. . . . There's only one way out—and that's *through* the dark woods. *You must change your life.*

—**PHIL COUSINEAU**
writer/filmmaker

For the past thirty-three years, I have looked in the mirror every morning and asked myself: "If today were the last day of my life, would I want to do what I am about to do today?" And whenever the answer has been "No" for too many days in a row, I know I need to change something.

—**STEVE JOBS**
entrepreneur

We didn't evolve to be constantly content. Contented *Australopithecus afarensis* got eaten before passing on their genes.

—**TIM MINCHIN**
musician/comedian

People wish to be settled; only as far as they are unsettled is there any hope for them.

–RALPH WALDO EMERSON
essayist

If . . . you won't let yourself get away from that one straight line, oh, my goodness, that's too horrible to even think about.

–WES MONTGOMERY
jazz musician

new beginnings

What is that feeling when you're driving away from people and they recede on the plain till you see their specks dispersing?—it's the too-huge world vaulting us, and it's good-by. But we lean forward to the next crazy venture beneath the skies.

–JACK KEROUAC
writer

Take all the rules away. How can we live if we don't change?

–BEYONCÉ
entertainer

new
beginnings

I live in the space between chaos and shape. I walk the line that continually threatens to lose its tautness under me, dropping me into the dark pit where there is no meaning. At other times the line is so wired that it lights up the soles of my feet, gradually my whole body, until I am my own beacon, and I see then the beauty of newly created worlds, a form that is not random. A new beginning.

–JEANETTE WINTERSON
writer

I was surprised, as always, by how easy the act of leaving was, and how good it felt. The world was suddenly rich with possibility.

–JON KRAKAUER
writer/mountaineer

No one expected me. Everything awaited me.

–PATTI SMITH
musician/writer

. . . .

For last year's words belong to last
   year's language
And next year's words await another
   voice....
And to make an end is to make a
   beginning.

–T. S. ELIOT
poet

. . . .

O

opportunity

outlook

People will try to tell you that all the great opportunities have been snapped up. In reality, the world changes every second, blowing new opportunities in all directions, including yours.

–KEN HAKUTA
inventor

Leave the door open for the unknown, the door into the dark. That's where the most important things come from, where you yourself came from, and where you will go.

–REBECCA SOLNIT
writer

Business opportunities are like buses, there's always another one coming.

–RICHARD BRANSON
entrepreneur

opportunity

outlook

....

Bill Gates said, "When you look back on what happened in a two-year period, you always think nothing has changed. But when you look at ten years, everything's changed." I find that to be so true. A two-year period just seems like *Mmm, we're stuck*. But ten years is unrecognizable.

–BILL MAHER
humorist

....

You do not notice changes in what is always before you.

–COLETTE
writer

....

The truth about the world, he said, is that anything is possible. Had you not seen it all from birth and thereby bled it of its strangeness it would appear to you for what it is, a hat trick in a medicine show, a fevered dream, a trance bepopulate with chimeras having neither analogue nor precedent, an itinerant carnival, a migratory tentshow whose ultimate destination after many a pitch in many a mudded field is unspeakable and calamitous beyond reckoning.

–**CORMAC MCCARTHY**
writer

Life . . . is about not knowing, having to change, taking the moment and making the best of it, without knowing what's going to happen next. Delicious ambiguity.

–**GILDA RADNER**
comedian

outlook
....

One's destination is never a place but rather a new way of looking at things.

–HENRY MILLER
writer

To live is to change, and to be perfect is to change often.

–JOHN HENRY NEWMAN
cardinal/theologian

Jumping from boulder to boulder and never falling, with a heavy pack, is easier than it sounds; you just can't fall when you get into the rhythm of the dance.

–JACK KEROUAC
writer

I guess it's true what they say: if you wait long enough, everything changes.

–JUNOT DÍAZ
writer

I can choose either to be a victim of the world or an adventurer in search of treasure. It's all a question of how I view my life.

–PAULO COELHO
writer

Remember, when someone says "you've changed," it usually just means you've stopped living your life their way.

–RICKY GERVAIS
comedian

Change is rarely straightforward. . . . Sometimes it's as complex as chaos theory and as slow as evolution. Even things that seem to happen suddenly arise from deep roots in the past or from long-dormant seeds.

–REBECCA SOLNIT
writer

The Potato seems like a Romantic (organic) object; . . . you can watch it growing if you don't eat it. It is going to change—grow, rot, disappear. A pebble is like a Classical thing—it changes little if any. . . . If it was big you could keep the dead down with it. . . .
The Classical idea is not around much anymore.

–WILLEM DE KOONING
artist

outlook

P

paradoxes

past

*positive side
of change*

possibilities

preparation

present

The more things change, the more they stay the same.

–ALPHONSE KARR
critic

I have noticed that even those who assert that everything is predestined and that we can change nothing about it still look both ways before they cross the street.

–STEPHEN HAWKING
physicist

The decisive moment in human evolution is perpetual.

–FRANZ KAFKA
writer

paradoxes

Ceaseless change is the only constant thing in nature.

–JOHN CANDEE DEAN
writer

If we want things to stay as they are, things will have to change.

–GIUSEPPE TOMASI DI LAMPEDUSA
writer

There's nothing so stable as change.

–BOB DYLAN
musician

We stand in relation to the past very much like the cow in the meadow—endlessly chewing the cud. It is not something finished and done with, as we sometimes fondly imagine, but something alive, constantly changing, and perpetually with us. But the future too is with us perpetually, and alive and constantly changing.

–HENRY MILLER
writer

It's no use going back to yesterday, because I was a different person then.

–LEWIS CARROLL
writer/mathematician

The past, like the future, is indefinite and exists only as a spectrum of possibilities.

–STEPHEN HAWKING
physicist

*positive side
of change*

Change in all things is sweet.

—**ARISTOTLE**
philosopher

Some changes may look negative on the surface but you will soon realize that space is being created in your life for something new to emerge.

—**ECKHART TOLLE**
writer

Continuity in everything is unpleasant.

—**BLAISE PASCAL**
mathematician/philosopher

If you're doing something you've never done before, it's easier to feel more relaxed about it. When you're doing something you have done before, and you can't make it any better, then it starts the worry.

—**ORNETTE COLEMAN**
jazz musician

The transformation of the heart is a wondrous thing, no matter how you land there.

–PATTI SMITH
musician/writer

positive side of change

In me there have always been two fools, among others, one asking nothing better than to stay where he is and the other imagining that life might be slightly less horrible a little further on.

–SAMUEL BECKETT
writer

People who can change and change again are so much more reliable and happier than those who can't.

–STEPHEN FRY
comedian

There is a certain relief in change, even though it be from bad to worse; as I have found in traveling in a stage coach, that it is often a comfort to shift one's position, and be bruised in a new place.

–WASHINGTON IRVING
writer

I saw that my life was a vast glowing empty page and I could do anything I wanted.

–JACK KEROUAC
writer

If you over-plan, you close the door on possibilities.

–PATTI SMITH
musician/writer

To be hopeful, to embrace one possibility after another—that is surely the basic instinct. . . . Time to move out into the glorious debris. Time to take this life for what it is.

–BARBARA KINGSOLVER
writer

possibilities

possibilities

I see it all perfectly; there are two possible situations—one can do either this or that. My honest opinion and my friendly advice is this: Do it or do not do it—you will regret both.

–SØREN KIERKEGAARD
philosopher

I suspect the truth is that we are waiting, all of us, against insurmountable odds, for something extraordinary to happen to us.

–KHALED HOSSEINI
writer

I'm making space for the unknown future to fill up my life with yet-to-come surprises.

–ELIZABETH GILBERT
writer

Man must be prepared for every event of life, for there is nothing that is durable.

–MENANDER
writer

It is a bad plan that admits of no modification.

–PUBLILIUS SYRUS
writer

preparation

The water you touch in a river is the last of that which has passed, and the first of that which is coming. Thus it is with time present.

–LEONARDO DA VINCI
inventor/artist

present

137

present

The past alone is truly real: the present is but a painful, struggling birth into the immutable being of what is no longer.

–BERTRAND RUSSELL
philosopher

The present is the ever-moving shadow that divides yesterday from tomorrow. In that lies hope.

–FRANK LLOYD WRIGHT
architect

It is the insertion of man with his limited life span that transforms the continuously flowing stream of sheer change . . . into time as we know it.

–HANNAH ARENDT
philosopher

Fixity is always momentary. It is an equilibrium, at once precarious and perfect, that lasts the space of an instant: a flickering of the light, the appearance of a cloud.

–OCTAVIO PAZ
writer

present
....

I can't change anything now. I can't afford to regret. That life is simply gone now, and I can't regret its passing. I have to live in the present. The life back then is gone just as surely—it's as remote to me as if it had happened to somebody I read about in a nineteenth-century novel. I don't spend more than five minutes a month in the past. The past really *is* a foreign country, and they do do things differently there.

–**RAYMOND CARVER**
writer

We are always acting on what has just finished happening. It happened at least one thirtieth of a second ago. We think we're in the present, but we aren't. The present we know is only a movie of the past.

–**KEN KESEY**
writer

Q

quantum leaps

In a very real sense, *tomorrow is now*.

–ELEANOR ROOSEVELT
humanitarian

I used to think the future was solid or fixed, something you inherited like an old building that you move into. . . . But it's not. The future is not fixed, it's fluid. You can build your own building, or hut or condo, whatever.

–BONO
singer

The future will soon be a thing of the past.

–GEORGE CARLIN
comedian

quantum leaps

....

The future's main characteristic is its basic uncertainty, no matter how high a degree of probability prediction may attain. In other words, we are dealing with matters that never were, that are not yet, and that may well never be.

–HANNAH ARENDT
philosopher

Yesterday's weirdness is tomorrow's reason why.

–HUNTER S. THOMPSON
journalist

I have no doubt that in reality the future will be vastly more surprising than anything I can imagine. Now my own suspicion is that the Universe is not only queerer than we suppose, but queerer than we can suppose.

–J.B.S. HALDANE
scientist

The future is inevitable and precise, but it may not occur. God lurks in the gaps.

–JORGE LUIS BORGES
writer

Never let the future disturb you. You will meet it, if you have to, with the same weapons of reason which today arm you against the present.

–MARCUS AURELIUS
philosopher/emperor

The only thing we know about the future is that it is going to be different.

–PETER DRUCKER
management consultant

quantum leaps

quantum leaps

Anything can happen, but it usually doesn't.

–ROBERT BENCHLEY
humorist

The future is called "perhaps," which is the only possible thing to call the future. And the important thing is not to allow that to scare you.

–TENNESSEE WILLIAMS
writer

When you cut into the present, the future leaks out.

–WILLIAM BURROUGHS
writer

The future is not google-able.

–WILLIAM GIBSON
writer

I like the dreams of the future better than the history of the past. So good night. I will dream on. . . .

–THOMAS JEFFERSON
president

R

resisting change

risk taking

Humans are allergic to change. They love to say, "We've always done it this way." I try to fight that. That's why I have a clock on my wall that runs counter-clockwise.

–REAR ADMIRAL GRACE HOPPER
computer scientist

When we resist change, it's called suffering. But when we can completely let go and not struggle against it, when we can embrace the groundlessness of our situation and relax into its dynamic quality, that's called enlightenment.

–PEMA CHÖDRÖN
nun/teacher

resisting change

To play it safe is not to play.

–ROBERT ALTMAN
film director

It seems hardly proper to write of life without once mentioning happiness; so we shall let the reader answer this question for himself: who is the happier man, he who has braved the storm of life and lived or he who has stayed securely on shore and merely existed?

–HUNTER S. THOMPSON
journalist

Only those who will risk going too far can possibly find out how far one can go.

–T. S. ELIOT
poet

No one is ever safe. So why not live as much as you can?

–RITA MAE BROWN
writer

Fortune sides with him who dares.

–VIRGIL
poet

If everything seems under control, you're just not going fast enough.

–MARIO ANDRETTI
race car driver

Taking one's chances is like taking a bath, because sometimes you end up feeling comfortable and warm, and sometimes there is something terrible lurking around that you cannot see until it is too late and you can do nothing else but scream and cling to a plastic duck.

–LEMONY SNICKET
writer

Playing it safe will always end in disaster.

–BANKSY
graffiti artist

S

second chances

seeking change

stagnation

surprises

We all have big changes in our lives that are more or less a second chance.

–HARRISON FORD
actor

Second chances do come your way. Like trains, they arrive and depart regularly. Recognizing the ones that matter is the trick.

–JILL A. DAVIS
writer

. . . .

You just stay here in this one corner of the Forest waiting for the others to come to *you*. Why don't you go to *them* sometimes?

–A. A. MILNE
writer

second chances

. . . .

seeking change

. . . .

seeking change

....

All of us, from time to time, need a plunge into freedom and novelty. After that, routine and discipline will seem delightful by contrast.

–ANDRÉ MAUROIS
writer

Get and stay out of your comfort zone. I believe that not much happens of any significance when we're in our comfort zone. I hear people say, "But I'm concerned about security." My response to that is simple: "Security is for cadavers."

–BOB PARSONS
entrepreneur

There are times to stay put, and what you want will come to you, and there are times to go out into the world and find such a thing for yourself.

–LEMONY SNICKET
writer

[We] arrive where we started
And know the place for the first time.

–T. S. ELIOT
poet

Why do you go away? So that you can come back.
So that you can see the place you came from with
new eyes and extra colors. And the people there
see you differently, too. Coming back to where you
started is not the same as never leaving.

–TERRY PRATCHETT
writer

We keep moving forward, opening up new doors
and doing new things, because we are curious . . .
and curiosity keeps leading us down new paths.

–WALT DISNEY
entrepreneur

stagnation

....

Listen. To live is to be marked. To live is to change, to acquire the words of a story, and that is the only celebration we mortals really know. In perfect stillness, frankly, I've only found sorrow.

–BARBARA KINGSOLVER
writer

All we can hope is that we will fail better. That we won't succumb to fear of the unknown. That we will not fall prey to the easy enchantments of repeating what may have worked in the past.

–DANI SHAPIRO
writer

Life is a process of becoming, a combination of states we have to go through. Where people fail is that they wish to elect a state and remain in it. This is a kind of death.

–ANAÏS NIN
writer

He who rejects change is the architect of decay. The only human institution which rejects progress is the cemetery.

–HAROLD WILSON
British prime minister

stagnation

So many people live within unhappy circumstances and yet will not take the initiative to change their situation because they are conditioned to a life of security, conformity, and conservatism, all of which may appear to give one peace of mind, but in reality nothing is more damaging to the adventurous spirit within a man than a secure future.

–CHRIS MCCANDLESS
(as quoted by Jon Krakauer)

After living with their dysfunctional behavior for so many years (a sunk cost if there ever was one), people become invested in defending their dysfunctions rather than changing them.

–MARSHALL GOLDSMITH
leadership coach/writer

The man who never alters his opinion is like standing water, and breeds reptiles of the mind.

–WILLIAM BLAKE
poet

You'll find people where their conditions aren't changing in any way, it's rather rare for them to be happy.

–DAVID ATTENBOROUGH
naturalist

It is the fixed that horrifies us, the fixed that assails us with the tremendous force of mindlessness. The fixed is a Mason jar, and we can't beat it open. . . . The fixed is a world without fire—dead flint, dead tinder, and nowhere a spark. It is motion without direction, force without power, the aimless procession of caterpillars round the rim of a vase, and I hate it because at any moment I myself might step to that charmed and glistening thread.

–ANNIE DILLARD
writer

In nature every moment is new; the past is always swallowed and forgotten. . . . Life is a series of surprises.

–RALPH WALDO EMERSON
essayist

Sometimes not having any idea where we're going works out better than we could possibly have imagined.

–ANN PATCHETT
writer

I'm hoping to be astonished tomorrow by I don't know what.

–JIM HARRISON
writer

I don't know where I'm going from here but I promise it won't be boring.

–DAVID BOWIE
musician

T

time

time for change

transience

The present flowed by them like a stream. The tree rustled. It had made music before they were born, and would continue after their deaths, but its song was of the moment. The moment had passed. The tree rustled again. Their senses were sharpened, and they seemed to apprehend life. Life passed. The tree rustled again.

–E. M. FORSTER
writer

Since time is a continuum, the moment is always different.

–HERBIE HANCOCK
musician

Maybe that's what life is . . . a wink of the eye and winking stars.

–JACK KEROUAC
writer

time for change

. . . .

Where does discontent start? You are warm enough, but you shiver. You are fed, yet hunger gnaws you. You have been loved, but your yearning wanders in new fields. And to prod all these there's time, the bastard Time.

–JOHN STEINBECK
writer

. . . .

There are lots of things a warrior can do at a certain time which he couldn't do years before. Those things themselves did not change; what changed was his idea of himself.

–CARLOS CASTANEDA
writer

. . . .

When people are ready to, they change. They never do it before then, and sometimes they die before they get around to it. You can't make them change if they don't want to, just like when they do want to, you can't stop them.

–ANDY WARHOL
artist

....

Because things are the way they are, things will not stay the way they are.

–BERTOLT BRECHT
writer

The person you are right now is as transient, as fleeting and as temporary as all the people you've ever been.

–DAN GILBERT
Harvard psychologist

time for change

transience

transience

The child's world is made not of clay, to last, but of clouds.

–NIKOS KAZANTZAKIS
writer

A permanent state of transition is man's most noble condition.

–JUAN RAMÓN JIMÉNEZ
writer

Transience makes a ghost out of each experience.
There was never a dawn that did not drop down into
noon, never a noon which did not fade into evening,
and never an evening that did not get buried in the
graveyard of the night.

–JOHN O'DONOHUE
poet/philosopher

There are no permanent changes because change itself
is permanent.

–RALPH L. WOODS
writer

Is there anything we know more intimately than the
fleetingness of time, the transience of each and every
moment?

–REBECCA GOLDSTEIN
philosopher

No permanence is ours; we are a wave
That flows to fit whatever form it finds.

–HERMANN HESSE
writer

On the edge of the city you'll see us and then
We come with the dust and we go with the wind

–WOODY GUTHRIE
musician

Would that life were like the shadow cast by a wall or a tree, but it is like the shadow of a bird in flight.

–TALMUD

U

unchanging center

unexpected

To watch is to observe without choice, to see yourself as you are without any movement of desire to change, which is an extremely arduous thing to do; but that doesn't mean that you are going to remain in your present state. You do not know what will happen if you see yourself as you are without wishing to bring about a change in that which you see. Do you understand?

—JIDDU KRISHNAMURTI
philosopher

unchanging center

Change your leaves, keep intact your roots.

—VICTOR HUGO
writer

unchanging center

Accident ruled every corner of the universe except the chambers of the human heart.

–DAVID GUTERSON
writer

It partook . . . of eternity . . . there is a coherence in things, a stability; something, she meant, is immune from change, and shines out (she glanced at the window with its ripple of reflected lights) in the face of the flowing, the fleeting, the spectral, like a ruby; so that again tonight she had the feeling she had had once today, already, of peace, of rest. Of such moments, she thought, the thing is made that endures.

–VIRGINIA WOOLF
writer

He who does not expect will not find out the unexpected, for it is trackless and unexplored.

–HERACLITUS
philosopher

None of us knows what the next change is going to be, what unexpected opportunity is just around the corner, waiting . . . to change all the tenor of our lives.

–KATHLEEN THOMPSON NORRIS
writer

Fate is like a strange, unpopular restaurant filled with odd little waiters who bring you things you never asked for and don't always like.

–LEMONY SNICKET
writer

unexpected

V

verities

If you can't change your fate, change your attitude.

–AMY TAN
writer

The secret is to move with the punch.

–JAKE LAMOTTA
boxer

Creation is something that is most holy; that's the most sacred thing in life and if you have made a mess of your life, change it. Change it today, not tomorrow.

–JIDDU KRISHNAMURTI
philosopher

Change before you have to.

–JACK WELCH
business executive

verities

Nothing is built on stone; all is built on sand, but we must build as if the sand were stone.

–JORGE LUIS BORGES
writer

There's no use in comparing one's feelings between one day and the next: you must allow a reasonable interval, for the *direction* of change to show itself. Sit on the beach, and watch the waves for a few seconds: you will say "the tide is coming in": watch half a dozen successive waves, and you may say "the last is the lowest: it is going out": wait a quarter of an hour, and compare its *average* place with what it was at first, and you will say "no, it is coming in, after all."

–LEWIS CARROLL
writer/mathematician

Never play anything the same way twice.

–BIX BEIDERBECKE
(ALSO ATTRIBUTED TO
LOUIS ARMSTRONG)
jazz musician

. . . .

"Since we cannot change reality, let us change the eyes which see reality," says one of my favorite Byzantine mystics. I did this when a child; I do it now as well in the most creative moments of my life.

–NIKOS KAZANTZAKIS
writer

Life is like underwear, should be changed twice a day.

–RAY BRADBURY
writer

. . . .

If you don't go, you'll never know. I tell that to my kids.

–ROBERT DE NIRO
actor

. . . .

Make no mistake. You can change things. Don't believe anyone who tells you that you can't. Here's how to do it. Question everything. Take nothing for granted. Argue with all received ideas. Don't respect what doesn't deserve respect. Speak your mind. Don't censor yourselves. Use your imagination. And express what it tells you to express.

–SALMAN RUSHDIE
writer

The whole future lies in uncertainty: live immediately.

–SENECA
philosopher

Change your life today. Don't gamble on the future, act now, without delay.

–SIMONE DE BEAUVOIR
writer

verities

verities

. . . .

I think if you do something and it turns out pretty good, then you should go do something else wonderful, not dwell on it for too long. Just figure out what's next.

–STEVE JOBS
entrepreneur

Can't say it often enough—change your hair, change your life.

–THOMAS PYNCHON
writer

Live the questions.

–RAINER MARIA RILKE
writer

If you want to change the world, change yourself.

–TOM ROBBINS
writer

Buy the ticket, take the ride.

–**HUNTER S. THOMPSON**
journalist

It was a rule I had learned my first year working in the Forest Service—when exhausted and feeling sorry for yourself, at least change socks.

–**NORMAN MACLEAN**
writer

Time changes everything except something within us which is always surprised by change.

—**THOMAS HARDY**
writer

It is likely that some troubles will befall us; but it is not a present fact. How often has the unexpected happened! How often has the expected never come to pass!

—**SENECA**
philosopher

Getting started, keeping going, getting started again— in art and in life, it seems to me this is the essential rhythm not only of achievement but of survival, the ground of convinced action, the basis of self-esteem, and the guarantee of credibility in your lives, credibility to yourselves as well as to others.

—**SEAMUS HEANEY**
poet

Only to the extent that we expose ourselves over and over to annihilation can that which is indestructible be found in us.

–PEMA CHÖDRÖN
nun/teacher

Those who cannot change their minds cannot change anything.

–GEORGE BERNARD SHAW
playwright

If you change the way you look at things, the things you look at change.

–WAYNE W. DYER
motivational speaker

W
welcoming change

You have to move freely into the arena, not just to wait for the perfect situation, the perfect moment. . . . If you have to make a mistake, it's better to make a mistake of action than one of inaction. If I had the opportunity again, I would take chances.

–FEDERICO FELLINI
film director

To keep our faces toward change and behave like free spirits in the presence of fate is strength undefeatable.

–HELEN KELLER
humanitarian

"Things don't stay the way they are," said Finnerty. "It's too entertaining to try to change them."

–KURT VONNEGUT
writer

welcoming change

welcoming change

Weep not that the world changes—did it keep
A stable, changeless state, 'twere cause indeed to
weep.

–WILLIAM CULLEN BRYANT
writer

If we do not find anything pleasant, at least we shall
find something new.

**–VOLTAIRE
(FRANÇOIS-MARIE AROUET)**
writer

Things are going to happen whether I know why they
happen or not. It just gets more complicated when
you stick yourself into it. You don't find out why
things move. You let them move; you watch them
move; you stop them from moving: you start them
moving. But you don't sit around and try to figure out
why there's movement.

–BOB DYLAN
musician

Everything flows and nothing stays.

—**HERACLITUS**
philosopher

Life is never a material, a substance to be molded. If you want to know, life is the principle of self-renewal, it is constantly renewing and remaking and changing and transfiguring itself, it is infinitely beyond your or my obtuse theories about it.

—**BORIS PASTERNAK**
writer

You can't make anything go anywhere. It just happens.

–THELONIOUS MONK
jazz musician

The current of the river of life moves us. Awareness of life, beauty and happiness is the current of the river.

–AGNES MARTIN
artist

Life is an improvisation. You have no idea what's going to happen next and you are mostly just making things up as you go along.

–STEPHEN COLBERT
comedian/talk show host

At the highest level, I'm letting something happen—
I'm not causing it to happen. . . . We're opening a door,
but we're not responsible for what comes through it.

–JERRY GARCIA
musician

Joy is new possibilities; it points toward the future.
Joy is living on the razor's edge; happiness promises
satisfaction of one's present state, a fulfillment of old
longings. Joy is the thrill of new continents to explore;
it is an unfolding of life.

–ROLLO MAY
psychologist

*welcoming
change*

Life is a lot like jazz . . . it's best when you improvise.

–GEORGE GERSHWIN
composer

Whatever the present moment contains, accept it as if you had chosen it. Always work with it, not against it.

–ECKHART TOLLE
writer

X

xenophobia/
xenophilia

Now is the dramatic moment of fate, Watson, when you hear a step upon the stair which is walking into your life, and you know not whether for good or ill.

–ARTHUR CONAN DOYLE
writer

Our lot is to learn and to be hurled into inconceivable new worlds.

–CARLOS CASTANEDA
writer

My favorite thing is to go where I've never been.

–DIANE ARBUS
photographer

xenophobia/ xenophilia

Be patient toward all that is unsolved in your heart and try to love the questions themselves like locked rooms and like books that are written in a very foreign tongue.

–RAINER MARIA RILKE
writer

If you don't know it's impossible it's easier to do. And because nobody's done it before, they haven't made up rules to stop anyone doing that again, yet.

–NEIL GAIMAN
writer

The job is to seek mystery, evoke mystery, plant a garden in which strange plants grow and mysteries bloom. The need for mystery is greater than the need for an answer.

–KEN KESEY
writer

xenophobia/ xenophilia

Y
you

I waited a long time out in the world before I gave myself permission to fail. Please don't even bother asking. Don't bother telling the world you are ready. Show it. Do it.

–PETER DINKLAGE
actor

It is the greatest mistake to think that man is always one and the same. A man is never the same for long. He is continually changing. He seldom remains the same even for half an hour.

–G. I. GURDJIEFF
mystic/philosopher

I change every day, change my patterns, my concepts, my interpretations. I am a series of moods and sensations.

–ANAÏS NIN
writer

you

you
....

Can one know one's self? Is one ever somebody?
I don't know of anything about it anymore. It now
seems to me that one changes from day to day and
that every few years one becomes a new being.

–GEORGE SAND
writer

Each day, we wake slightly altered, and the person we
were yesterday is dead.

–JOHN UPDIKE
writer

I am not what I once was.

–HORACE
poet

"I do know my own mind," protested Anne. "The trouble is, my mind changes and then I have to get acquainted with it all over again."

–L. M. MONTGOMERY
writer

I am not now
That which I have been.

–LORD BYRON
poet

You're always you, and that don't change, and you're always changing, and there's nothing you can do about it.

–NEIL GAIMAN
writer

There is nothing like returning to a place that remains unchanged to see the ways that you yourself have changed.

–NELSON MANDELA
statesman

you

you

People change and forget to tell each other.

–LILLIAN HELLMAN
writer

The simplest questions are the most profound.
Where were you born?
Where is your home?
Where are you going?
What are you doing?
Think about these once in a while, and watch your answers change.

–RICHARD BACH
writer

The Brahmin . . . had left his family and came back with his hair turned white. When his neighbors recognized him, they called out: "The man who once left us is still alive?" But the Brahmin answered: "I resemble him, but am no longer the same."

–SENG-CHAO
monk/philosopher

Some changes happen deep down inside of you. And the truth is, only you know about them. Maybe that's the way it's supposed to be.

–JUDY BLUME
writer

Z

zero hour

Life is a moveable feast . . . a tour in a post chaise, but who's to be considered as moving, it or you? The answer is—quick over the abyss, and be damned to being. Start *doing*.

–HORTENSE CALISHER
writer

A great change in life is like a cold bath in winter—we all hesitate at the first plunge.

–LETITIA ELIZABETH LANDON
poet

Change almost never fails because it's too early. It almost always fails because it's too late.

–SETH GODIN
writer/entrepreneur

If you're offered a seat on a rocket ship, don't ask what seat. Just get on.

–SHERYL SANDBERG
technology executive

zero hour

If we wait until we're ready, we'll be waiting for the rest of our lives.

–LEMONY SNICKET
writer

Change is good . . . you go first.

**–TOM FELTENSTEIN AND
MAC ANDERSON**
business executives/writers

There's a point when you go with what you've got. Or you don't go.

–JOAN DIDION
writer

A kind of light spread out from her. And everything changed color. And the world opened out. And a day was good to awaken to. And there were no limits to anything. And the people of the world were good and handsome. And I was not afraid any more.

–JOHN STEINBECK
writer

MORE QUOTABLE WISDOM FROM KATHRYN & ROSS PETRAS

Hundreds of pithy words, thoughts, and ideas to inspire dreamers and doers.

The best things men and women over 60 have said about how to love, work, laugh, and live—really live.

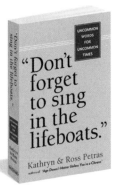

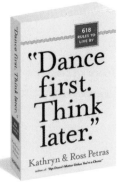

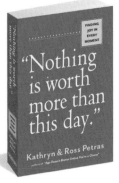

It's tough out there, but you're not alone—take it from people who've graduated from the school of hard knocks.

The greatest advice for this puzzling business of being alive, with 618 unexpected rules to live by.

There is always something to celebrate—and these writers, scientists, athletes, and others show you how to see it.